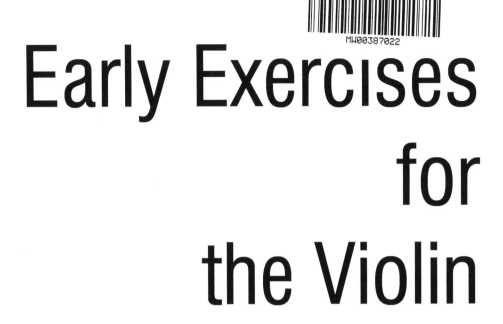

Early Exercises for the Violin

by Cassia Harvey

CHP292

©2016 by C. Harvey Publications All Rights Reserved.

www.charveypublications.com

Finger Exercise 1

©2016 C. Harvey Publications All Rights Reserved.

Rhythm 1
"Peanut-butter Sandwich"

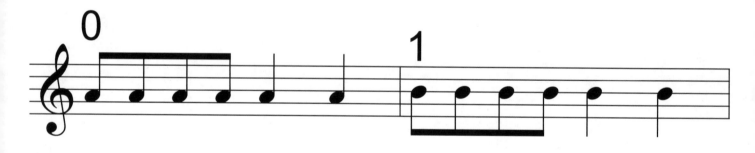

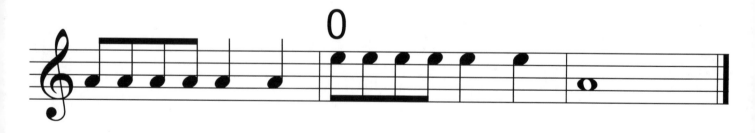

©2016 C. Harvey Publications All Rights Reserved.

String Crossing 1

©2016 C. Harvey Publications All Rights Reserved.

Finger Exercise 2

©2016 C. Harvey Publications All Rights Reserved.

Rhythm 2
"Peanut-butter Sandwich"

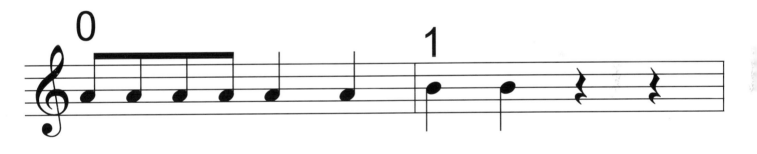

©2016 C. Harvey Publications All Rights Reserved.

String Crossing 2

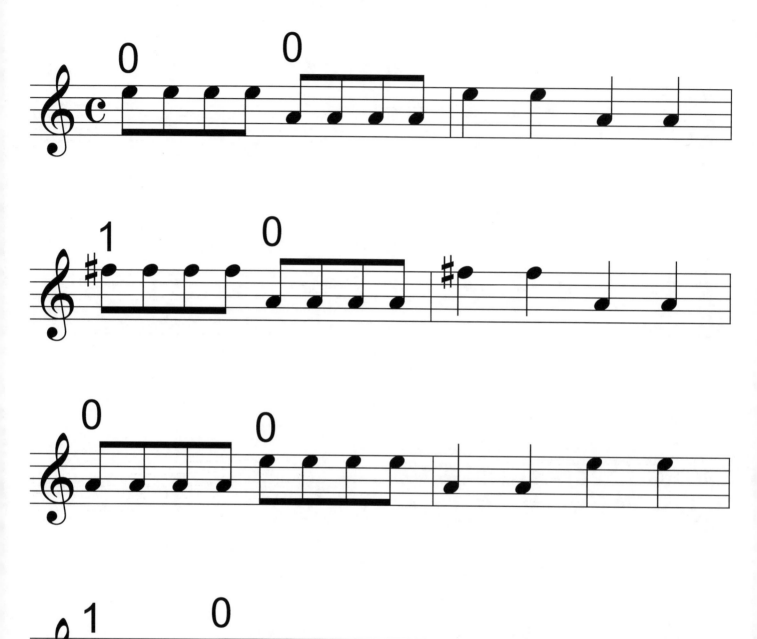

©2016 C. Harvey Publications All Rights Reserved.

Finger Exercise 3

©2016 C. Harvey Publications All Rights Reserved.

Rhythm 3
"Peanut-butter Sandwich"

©2016 C. Harvey Publications All Rights Reserved.

String Crossing 3

©2016 C. Harvey Publications All Rights Reserved.

Finger Exercise 4

©2016 C. Harvey Publications   All Rights Reserved.

Rhythm 4
"Long-Short-Short"

©2016 C. Harvey Publications All Rights Reserved.

String Crossing 4

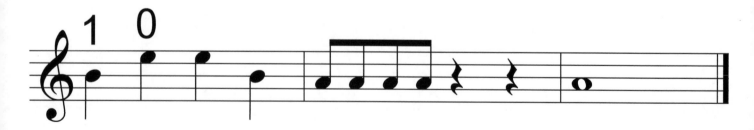

©2016 C. Harvey Publications All Rights Reserved.

Finger Exercise 5

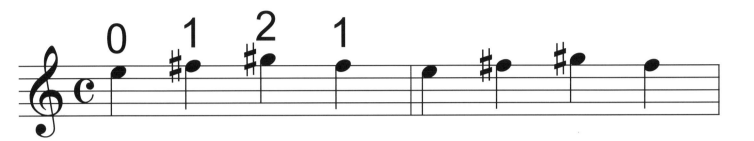

©2016 C. Harvey Publications All Rights Reserved.

Rhythm 5
"Long-Short-Short"

©2016 C. Harvey Publications All Rights Reserved.

String Crossing 5

©2016 C. Harvey Publications All Rights Reserved.

Finger Exercise 6

©2016 C. Harvey Publications All Rights Reserved.

Rhythm 6
"Long-Short-Short"

©2016 C. Harvey Publications All Rights Reserved.

String Crossing 6

©2016 C. Harvey Publications All Rights Reserved.

Finger Exercise 7

©2016 C. Harvey Publications   All Rights Reserved.

Rhythm 7
"Short-Short-Long"

©2016 C. Harvey Publications All Rights Reserved.

String Crossing 7

©2016 C. Harvey Publications All Rights Reserved.

Finger Exercise 8

©2016 C. Harvey Publications All Rights Reserved.

Rhythm 8
"Short-Short-Long"

©2016 C. Harvey Publications All Rights Reserved.

String Crossing 8

©2016 C. Harvey Publications All Rights Reserved.

Finger Exercise 9

©2016 C. Harvey Publications All Rights Reserved.

Rhythm 9
"Short-Short-Long"

©2016 C. Harvey Publications All Rights Reserved.

String Crossing 9

©2016 C. Harvey Publications All Rights Reserved.

Finger Exercise 10

©2016 C. Harvey Publications All Rights Reserved.

Rhythm 10
3 Beats in a Measure

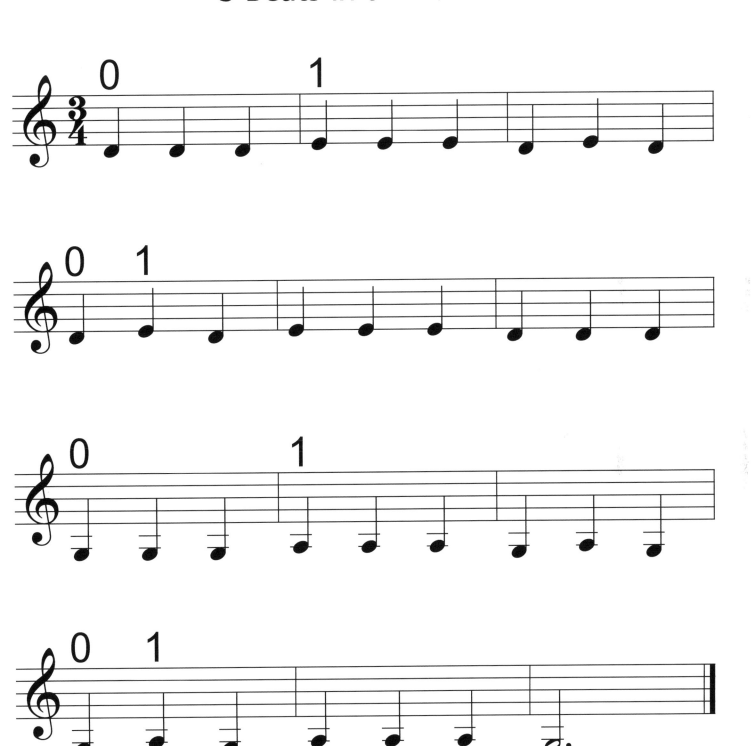

©2016 C. Harvey Publications All Rights Reserved.

String Crossing 10: Slurs

©2016 C. Harvey Publications All Rights Reserved.

Finger Exercise 11

©2016 C. Harvey Publications All Rights Reserved.

Rhythm 11
3 Beats in a Measure

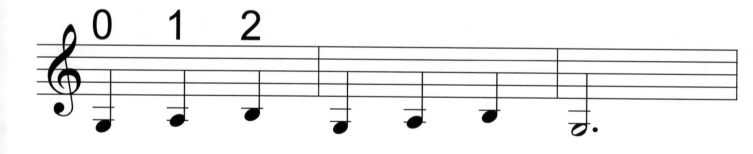

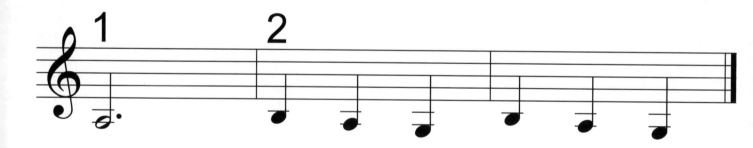

©2016 C. Harvey Publications All Rights Reserved.

String Crossing 11: Slurs

©2016 C. Harvey Publications All Rights Reserved.

Finger Exercise 12

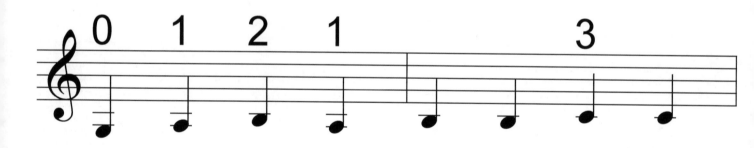

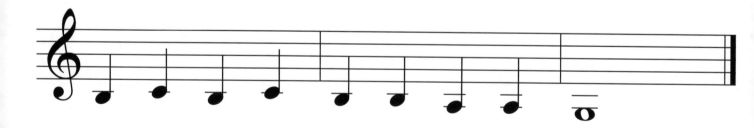

©2016 C. Harvey Publications All Rights Reserved.

Rhythm 12
3 Beats in a Measure

©2016 C. Harvey Publications All Rights Reserved.

String Crossing 12: Slurs

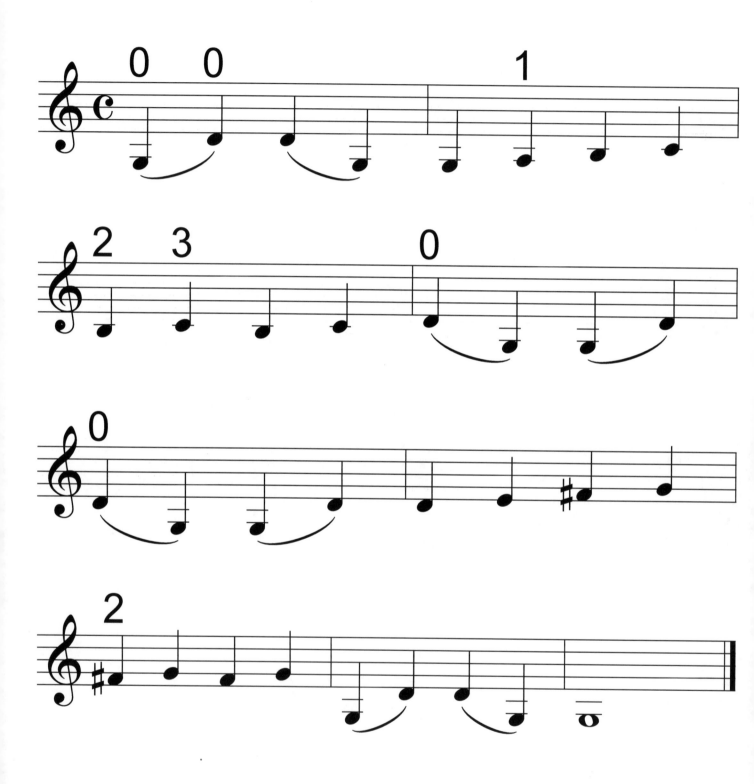

©2016 C. Harvey Publications All Rights Reserved.

Finger Exercise 13

©2016 C. Harvey Publications All Rights Reserved.

Rhythm 13
3 Beats in a Measure

©2016 C. Harvey Publications All Rights Reserved.

String Crossing 13: Slurs

©2016 C. Harvey Publications All Rights Reserved.

Finger Exercise 14: Low 2nd Finger

©2016 C. Harvey Publications All Rights Reserved.

Rhythm 14
Half Note Rhythms

©2016 C. Harvey Publications All Rights Reserved.

String Crossing 14: Slurs

©2016 C. Harvey Publications All Rights Reserved.

Finger Exercise 15: Low 2nd Finger

©2016 C. Harvey Publications All Rights Reserved.

Rhythm 15
Half Note Rhythms

©2016 C. Harvey Publications All Rights Reserved.

String Crossing 15: Slurs

©2016 C. Harvey Publications All Rights Reserved.

Finger Exercise 16: Low 2nd Finger

©2016 C. Harvey Publications All Rights Reserved.

Rhythm 16
Half Note Rhythms

©2016 C. Harvey Publications All Rights Reserved.

String Crossing 16: Slurs

©2016 C. Harvey Publications All Rights Reserved.

Finger Exercise 17: Low 2nd Finger

©2016 C. Harvey Publications All Rights Reserved.

Rhythm 17
Half Note Rhythms

©2016 C. Harvey Publications All Rights Reserved.

String Crossing 17: Slurs

©2016 C. Harvey Publications All Rights Reserved.

Finger Exercise 18: Low 2nd Finger

©2016 C. Harvey Publications All Rights Reserved.

Rhythm 18
Half Note Rhythms

©2016 C. Harvey Publications All Rights Reserved.

String Crossing 18: Slurs

©2016 C. Harvey Publications All Rights Reserved.

The Mary Had a Little Lamb Book for Violin

1. Mary Had a Little Lamb

2. Mary Had Some Whole Notes

©2006 C. Harvey Publications All Rights Reserved.

81705550R00033

Made in the USA
Lexington, KY
20 February 2018